What's Love Got to do with This...

MARY HALE

www.weareaps.com

Copyright © 2021 by Mary Hale

All rights reserved.

No portion of this book may be reproduced mechanically, electronically, or by any other means, including photocopying, without written permission of the publisher.

ISBN: 978-1-945145-70-4

This Book Belongs To

_____

DAY 1

Love Is...

"With all lowliness and meekness, with longsuffering, forbearing one another in love;" Ephesians 4:2 KJV

when another person's happiness is more important than yours

Loves Does What's Best!

DAY 2

Love Is...

"With all lowliness and meekness, with longsuffering, forbearing one another in love;" Ephesians 4:2 KJV

WHEN YOU FEEL SO COMFORTABLE THAT YOU CAN TALK ABOUT ANYTHING AND EVERYTHING... NO SECRETS, NO LIES

Loves Does What's Best!

DAY
3

Love Is...

"With all lowliness and meekness, with longsuffering, forbearing one another in love;" Ephesians 4:2 KJV

Letting go of the broken historical pieces of yesterday of how we thought life should be and learning to live in the story we are in now.

Loves Does What's Best!

DAY
4

Love Is...

"With all lowliness and meekness, with longsuffering, forbearing one another in love;" Ephesians 4:2 KJV

finding someone that is happy to love you and does not see love as being hard

Loves Does What's Best!

DAY 5

Love Is...

"With all lowliness and meekness, with longsuffering, forbearing one another in love;" Ephesians 4:2 KJV

loving someone with
the same feeling you
get when you see
your
favorite food

Loves Does What's Best!

DAY 6

Love Is...

"With all lowliness and meekness, with longsuffering, forbearing one another in love;" Ephesians 4:2 KJV

when we act from
our heart and not
from our pain

Loves Does What's Best!

DAY 7

L o v e   I s . . .

"With all lowliness and meekness, with longsuffering, forbearing one another in love;" Ephesians 4:2 KJV

a person who comes into your life by accident but stays on purpose

Loves Does What's Best!

DAY 8

Love Is...

"With all lowliness and meekness, with longsuffering, forbearing one another in love;" Ephesians 4:2 KJV

reminiscing about someone during a sad song

Loves Does What's Best!

DAY 9

Love Is...

"With all lowliness and meekness, with longsuffering, forbearing one another in love;" Ephesians 4:2 KJV

thinking of
someone when they
are thinking about
you

Loves Does What's Best!

DAY 10

Love Is...

"With all lowliness and meekness, with longsuffering, forbearing one another in love;" Ephesians 4:2 KJV

loaning someone your strength instead of reminding them of their weakness

Loves Does What's Best!

DAY 11

Love Is...

"With all lowliness and meekness, with longsuffering, forbearing one another in love;" Ephesians 4:2 KJV

Giving someone power to destroy you, but trusting them not to

Loves Does What's Best!

DAY 12

Love Is...

"With all lowliness and meekness, with longsuffering, forbearing one another in love;" Ephesians 4:2 KJV

A long-lasting romantic friendship

Loves Does What's Best!

DAY 13

Love Is...

"With all lowliness and meekness, with longsuffering, forbearing one another in love;" Ephesians 4:2 KJV

Never wanting to see the person you love hurt for any reason

Loves Does What's Best!

DAY 14

Love Is...

"With all lowliness and meekness, with longsuffering, forbearing one another in love;" Ephesians 4:2 KJV

being with
someone that will
give you their smile
when you cannot
find yours.

Loves Does What's Best!

DAY 15

Love Is...

"With all lowliness and meekness, with longsuffering, forbearing one another in love;" Ephesians 4:2 KJV

Hearing the music with someone and learning their lyrics

Loves Does What's Best!

DAY 16

Love Is...

"With all lowliness and meekness, with longsuffering, forbearing one another in love;" Ephesians 4:2 KJV

Two imperfect people coming together that refuse to give up on each other

Loves Does What's Best!

DAY 17

Love Is...

"With all lowliness and meekness, with longsuffering, forbearing one another in love;" Ephesians 4:2 KJV

Choosing someone to love again and again each and every day and in each and every way.

Loves Does What's Best!

DAY 18

Love Is...

"With all lowliness and meekness, with longsuffering, forbearing one another in love;" Ephesians 4:2 KJV

Overcoming obstacles, fights and challenges and fighting to be *together*

Loves Does What's Best!

DAY 19

Love Is...

"With all lowliness and meekness, with longsuffering, forbearing one another in love;" Ephesians 4:2 KJV

Love is holding on to
each other and
never letting go

Loves Does What's Best!

DAY 20

Love Is...

"With all lowliness and meekness, with longsuffering, forbearing one another in love;" Ephesians 4:2 KJV

Realizing that every minute and every hour was worth it because you spent the time together

Loves Does What's Best!

DAY 21

Love Is...

"With all lowliness and meekness, with longsuffering, forbearing one another in love;" Ephesians 4:2 KJV

a very powerful emotion, it allows us to face our thoughts *and issues*

Loves Does What's Best!

DAY 22

Love Is...

"With all lowliness and meekness, with longsuffering, forbearing one another in love;" Ephesians 4:2 KJV

being forgiving
rather than holding a
grudge

Loves Does What's Best!

DAY 23

Love Is...

"With all lowliness and meekness, with longsuffering, forbearing one another in love;" Ephesians 4:2 KJV

someone saying I have waited all my life to find you.

Loves Does What's Best!

DAY 24

Love Is...

"With all lowliness and meekness, with longsuffering, forbearing one another in love;" Ephesians 4:2 KJV

When you send me those texts and make me smile each time I read them

Loves Does What's Best!

DAY 25

Love Is...

"With all lowliness and meekness, with longsuffering, forbearing one another in love;" Ephesians 4:2 KJV

The way you
laugh and the
way you smile

Loves Does What's Best!

DAY 26

Love Is...

"With all lowliness and meekness, with longsuffering, forbearing one another in love;" Ephesians 4:2 KJV

You knowing that I did not choose you, my heart did.

Loves Does What's Best!

DAY 27

Love Is...

"With all lowliness and meekness, with longsuffering, forbearing one another in love;" Ephesians 4:2 KJV

A ghost hug from someone you love; you can't feel it, but it's there.

Loves Does What's Best!

DAY 28

Love Is...

"With all lowliness and meekness, with longsuffering, forbearing one another in love;" Ephesians 4:2 KJV

you fall in love with a person from out of the blue, at an unanticipated time.

Loves Does What's Best!

DAY 29

Love Is...

"With all lowliness and meekness, with longsuffering, forbearing one another in love;" Ephesians 4:2 KJV

when you find
both love and
friendship in
the same person

Loves Does What's Best!

DAY 30

Love Is...

"With all lowliness and meekness, with longsuffering, forbearing one another in love;" Ephesians 4:2 KJV

finding someone you want to annoy for the rest of your life

Loves Does What's Best!

Other Books by Mary Hale

Emotional Baggage
The Formation of My Walls
The Walls of My Heart
The Castle to My Heart

www.ingramcontent.com/pod-product-compliance
Lightning Source LLC
Chambersburg PA
CBHW070654050426
42451CB00008B/343